M000085118

Songs of My Heart & Tales from My Soul

Sakia G. Dixon

BK
ROYSTON
Publishing

BK Royston Publishing
P. O. Box 4321
Jeffersonville, IN 47131
502-802-5385
http://www.bkroystonpublishing.com
bkroystonpublishing@gmail.com

Cover Design Art: Gad of Elite Covers
Cover Photography: Chasing Memories Photography

ISBN-13: 978-1-951941-39-0

Printed in the United States of America

Dedication

To my leading ladies,

My mother who taught me, through song, that " He Looked Beyond My Faults."

My sister who reminds me, through words, that one should always "Encourage Yourself."

My daughter who impresses upon me, with every chord played on the black and white keys, to keep my heart filled with the "Joy, Joy, Joy" of the Lord.

Acknowledgements

With a joyful heart, I owe much gratitude to my Heavenly Father for all things.

To Tim, my husband and friend. Thank you for understanding my need to write at 1:00 am in the morning. Although the night light may have bothered you at times, you simply covered your head and encouraged me to "Keep writing."

My one and only girl, Kaiya. You are such a star in your own right. The day you acknowledged the story in me, I began to soar higher. I cannot wait to see where your light will lead you.

Thanks to my parents, Henry and Tonjai Gable, for allowing me to express myself freely and for helping to set the firm foundation of Christ within.

Much respect to the ladies who rock. My group of girlfriends "the Fab 5", co-workers, cousins, and Hearts of Beauty Sisters who uplift and motivate with each call and text message. Kimberli Dixon, my colleague, who said, "You should do it. People need to hear from you." Finally, I believed and I thank you.

Thanks to my church member, soror and friend, Vernet Clemons Nettles, who "did it first." I watched her journey and let her guide me in this venture.

To my awesome publisher, Julia Royston with BK Royston Publishing Company, thank you. What a pleasant experience for a first time author!

Lastly, I want to acknowledge you, the reader. This book is for you who remain faithful in the Christian walk and for you, who may stumble from time to time. There is no perfect person but there is one perfect God. Don't miss out on the best thing that could happen in a lifetime, a never ending relationship with Christ!

Blessings until the next time....

Table Of Contents

Introduction

Spending time with the Savior is such a relaxing thing to do. Listening to music and dancing is a close second behind. There is nothing like enjoying a lazy day on the back porch with music in my ears and a journal in my hands. My hope is that you experience unspeakable joy such as that with this 30 day devotional.

How you start the day is usually a great predictor of how the day will end. Starting the day with a strong cup of coffee and a personal gospel music concert is how I set the stage for success. Recently, my church began implementing early morning prayer. Adding corporate prayer to the morning routine, along with praise and worship, has elevated my relationship with God to even higher heights. Most mornings, a few words from a song would resonate within and lead me to seek God's message. After hearing the song over and over again, I would search His holy word and await a revelation. There was no plan or direction on my end. By simply yielding to the sweet voice of the holy spirit, my eyes and hands were guided to the right books, chapters, and verses for such a time as this. What you are holding in your hand is a segment of divine inspiration.

It is such a sweet peace to know God is always leading, even when we are traveling off the beaten path and headed towards the deep, dark valley.

Prayerfully, the messages in this book will assist in carrying you through many difficult days and seemingly, purposeless moments.

To reap the maximum benefit of this devotional, take it day by day. Read the devotional, study the word of God, listen to the suggested song, and journal your thoughts. Take it piece by piece, word by word and moment by moment.

Allow Him to speak to you through scriptures and songs. Since your conversations and revelations may differ from mine, and from time to time, begin to document your personal "Tales from the Heart" in the space provided for reflections. Once completed, dive in again. There will be new revelations with each read through. In spite of all that you may be experiencing, over the next 30 days choose to shift your focus to these things: Hope, Comfort, Freedom, Victory, and God's Unconditional Love.

Share with others so that they, too, can experience this transformational journey with you.

Sing your song.

Study your scripture.

Tell your tale.

Songs of Hope

What A Good God Is Our God!

God is good! God is good! God is good to me! My spirit leaps with joy at His goodness. Does His goodness tickle every one of your senses? Are you able to feel the warm embrace of God's gentle touch and His goodness in your emptiness? Can you smell His goodness despite the fumes of pending disaster? Can you taste His goodness during the sweet and the salty times in life? Can you see His goodness in bleak situations? Can you hear His goodness in His creation? Pause and place your focus on nothing else but the goodness that can only be found in God. Let go of the idea that God is only good when He blesses you, and focus on the premise that because God is good, everything He touches is good. Because you are one of His greatest creations, everything that touches you, surrounds you, or affects you will work out for your good.

God's goodness is found in all that is within Him. His love makes him GOOD. In Him alone, there is power, there is perfect peace, there is righteousness, there is healing, there is shelter, there is safety, there is security, there is protection, there is love. There is nothing lacking in God. He who created all things can take care of all things concerning you. Every situation you may deem as difficult, God is saying to you, "Just try Me. I will make it all good." When you are hungry, God is good. When you are sick, He's still good. When you are lonely, God is good. When you are tired, He's not, so He's still good. When you are lost, God is good. When you are *(you fill in the blank* _____*)*, God is good. There is nothing, not a thing that could happen to you where God cannot STILL be glorified for His goodness. When He created the heavens and earth, each and every part, God noted that it was good. He wants you to see and fully comprehend that He is good in all the minutiae and in the situations of life. If only, you would "taste" Him. Experience His presence. Escape with Him and enter His gardens and gates with praise. Your senses will thank you. Your life will be better for it. His goodness will outweigh every barrier in your way. You will come out singing and your soul rejoicing that God is good!

Study Your Scripture:

Psalm 34:8-14, NIV

"Taste and see that the Lord is good; blessed is the one who takes refuge in him. Fear the Lord, you his holy people, for those who fear him lack nothing. The lions may grow weak and hungry, but those who seek the Lord lack no good thing. Come, my children, listen to me; I will teach you the fear of the Lord. Whoever of you loves life and desires to see many good days, keep your tongue from evil and your lips from telling lies. Turn from evil and do good; seek peace and pursue it."

Sing Your Song:

"God is Good" by Regina Belle

Tell Your Tale:

Where have you seen God's goodness manifested
in your life?

_____
_____
_____
_____
_____
_____
_____
_____
_____
_____
_____
_____
_____
_____
_____
_____
_____
_____
_____
_____
_____

No Matter Your Start, You Can Still Win For Christ

The Bible is overwrought with stories, books, and examples of faith, trust, hope, and love. But Paul's letters to Timothy touch on every aspect of the four. Oh, how I love how Paul writes to Timothy and encourages him. It's nothing like receiving a "pat on the back" from someone you love and respect. Timothy was a young man but Paul, a disciple for Christ, had been on the battlefield for a long, long time. He knew the obstacles that would soon greet Timothy as he performed God's work. His words are purposed to support Timothy along his journey. With Paul's voice in his ear, Timothy could never forget that he had a calling on his life.

It seems as if Timothy had the perfect setup with two women who loved him unconditionally; perfect attendance in Sunday school and prayer meetings; regular intercession and fasting sessions in his home. Timothy was accustomed to Christ's soldiers interceding for him and warring on his behalf. He was used to working for the kingdom of God. To top it off, he had a good servant leader and friend in Paul, who was always praying for him. Despite those tools for success, he still had doubts. Was he too young for this mighty job? Did he possess the will to preach, teach, influence, and make a difference in the world? Timothy's journey demonstrates that no matter how good or bad the start, there will always be challenges along the way. Nevertheless, we must continue to fight the fight and stay the course.

I'm not naive enough to think that everyone was as fortunate to have the same upbringing as Timothy. Your story may read differently. Sunday may have been just another day in your household. Saying grace may have been optional and church attendance may have been only necessary for weddings, funerals, and Easter. If this narrative sounds like it could belong to you, it's no surprise if you may feel ill equipped for this work. Honey, please stop and recall the story of the encourager, Paul, who was a persecutor, a rebel, and a fighter until he had an encounter. And his life was forever changed.

If you are reading this, you've experienced at least one encounter and you desire another, another, and another. With each encounter, you will become a bigger, stronger advocate for Christ. If you don't have an encourager in your life, be an encourager to someone. You can continue to stay the course by being the cheerleader, the advocate, the uplifter, and a disciple for Christ. If you can't see your cheerleader in the natural, embrace the writings of Paul. Do not fear the gift that has been entrusted to you. Somebody prayed for you—I know that I did. So, don't dwell on your start. No matter if your start is likened to Timothy's or more like Paul's, this journey can be long and treacherous for anybody. Be steadfast in your efforts because your ending WILL be a win if your focus stays on Christ!

Study Your Scripture:

1 Timothy 4:1-16, NIV

"The Spirit clearly says that in later times some will abandon the faith and follow deceiving spirits and things taught by demons. Such teachings come through hypocritical liars, whose consciences have been seared as with a hot iron. They forbid people to marry and order them to abstain from certain foods, which God created to be received with thanksgiving by those who believe and who know the truth. For everything God created is good, and nothing is to be rejected if it is received with thanksgiving, because it is consecrated by the word of God and prayer. If you point these things out to the brothers and sisters, you will be a good minister of Christ Jesus, nourished on the truths of the faith and of the good teaching that you have followed. Have nothing to do with godless myths and old wives' tales; rather, train yourself to be godly. For physical training is of some value, but godliness has value for all things, holding promise for both the present life and the life to come. This is a trustworthy saying that deserves full acceptance. That is why we labor and strive, because we have put our hope in the living God, who is the Savior of all people, and especially of those who believe. Command and teach these things. Don't let anyone look down on you because you are young, but set an example for the believers in speech, in conduct, in love, in faith, and in purity. Until I come, devote yourself to the public reading of Scripture, to preaching and to teaching. Do not neglect your gift, which was given you through prophecy when the body of elders laid their hands on you. Be diligent in these matters; give yourself wholly to them, so that everyone may see your progress. Watch your life and doctrine closely. Persevere in them, because if you do, you will save both yourself and your hearers."

Sing Your Song:

"I'll Just Say Yes" by Brian Courtney Wilson

Tell Your Tale:

Take a moment. Take a deep breath. Now, describe your first encounter with God in detail. Where was it? What happened? What did you feel? What did you learn?

_____

_____

_____

_____

_____

_____

_____

_____

_____

_____

_____

_____

_____

_____

_____

_____

_____

_____

Nothing Is Yours And Yours Alone, Pass It On...

The carefree memories of high school are forever etched in my mind as a time of unbridled freedom. I took some losses (L's) and had quite a few wins (W's). Time at my performing arts magnet school was truly one of the best periods of my life. I have a memory box filled with pictures, notes, memorabilia (rings, headbands, movie tickets, etc.). Among all that fun stuff was a copy of one of my final assignments as a senior in high school. The teachers took this assignment quite seriously as it was a tradition for each senior to write a 'last will and testament' statement. The instructions were simple, not at all complex. We were asked to "give" something to the younger generation to help them reach our current level, which was the senior's last gift to the school.

The will could include actual items, advice, passwords, or even uniform items. I spent many hours deciding what I would leave to the younger classes. My final statement read that "I, Sakia Gable, am leaving nothing to the younger classes. I have to take with me all of the lessons I've learned and the information that has been given to me because I will need it in the years to come." Looking back, I bow in shame that I chose to leave nothing to the next generation. I have always been taught to get wisdom and understanding. As I have matured, I have gained both. I went to high school with no foreknowledge but learned so much that could have helped another along the way. It's the same with our Christian walk. As we live, we will gain a lot. It's up to us to tell and instruct the future generations. Our legacy is what we leave behind and the impact it will have on another.

If I had the opportunity to rewrite my high school last will and testament, I would leave tissues to wipe the tears of a classmate. I would leave smiles to share for those who were grieving or hurting during the day. I would leave prayers for a safe school environment at all times. I would leave scriptures in the bathroom stalls because I know some students may creep away for moments alone, and the words needed are often not found on the bathroom door. I accept this at face value. I came with nothing, and I'll leave with nothing. But while I'm here, I'll be sure to leave the world a little happier. Then, I will know that although I'm leaving with nothing, it's not because I did not give, and I did not gain. It is because I plan to leave my gains with others to be used to better God's kingdom. Friend, are you able to say the same?

Study Your Scripture:

Proverbs 4: 1-16, NIV

"Listen, my sons, to a father's instruction; pay attention and gain understanding. I give you sound learning, so do not forsake my teaching. For I too was a son to my father, still tender, and cherished by my mother. Then he taught me, and he said to me, "Take hold of my words with all your heart; keep my commands, and you will live. Get wisdom, get understanding; do not forget my words or turn away from them. Do not forsake wisdom, and she will protect you; love her, and she will watch over you. The beginning of wisdom is this: Get wisdom. Though it cost all you have, get understanding. Cherish her, and she will exalt you; embrace her, and she will honor you. She will give you a garland to grace your head and present you with a glorious crown. Listen, my son, accept what I say, and the years of your life will be many. I instruct you in the way of wisdom and lead you along straight paths. When you walk, your steps will not be hampered; when you run, you will not stumble. Hold on to instruction, do not let it go; guard it well, for it is your life. Do not set foot on the path of the wicked or walk in the way of evildoers. Avoid it, do not travel on it; turn from it and go on your way."

Sing Your Song:

"Withholding Nothing" by William McDowell

Tell Your Tale:

If you left this earth today, what do you hope that you have left during this life's journey? What more do you have to give to another?

_____
_____
_____
_____
_____
_____
_____
_____
_____
_____
_____
_____
_____
_____
_____
_____
_____
_____
_____

"It" Was Meant To Destroy,
You Were Meant To Overcome

What perilous times are we living in? Could anything more go wrong with this present life experience? An invasion of a deadly virus has infiltrated our world and upset our perfectly imbalanced lives. No one could have imagined or foretold the times we are currently facing. Schools are closed for a few weeks or...indefinitely. Government offices are shut down. The internet and television are besieged with nothing but bad news. The president of the free world does not appear to take "it" seriously. The nation's leaders in medicine are screaming that we are in a crisis and it's a pandemic, for goodness sake. "Take heed to our warnings and follow our mandates or this situation is destined to get worse." The people of the nation are confused, lost, and desperate for healing, answers, and peace. The doors of the church have always been open, until now. Weddings and graduations are postponed until further notice. Funerals must be private matters, only consisting of the immediate family. A mandate has gone out throughout the land that everyone must stay home at all cost, no matter the situation. If people must gather for one reason or another, no more than a group of ten is allowed, and everyone must remain at least six feet apart from another. Social distancing is what it's called. Of course, this sounds like a horrible sci-fi film gone wrong. Unfortunately, it's not. It's life, as we know it in the year 2020.

Scientists and medical professionals are working around the clock. They are sleeping in garages to quarantine themselves from their families. They are washing their hands until raw and bleeding all while trying to search for a cure, a vaccine, or an antidote for this horrible, terrible no good virus that has wrecked our nation. Stop right now and take note; there is good news. We KNOW the cure. We KNOW the vaccine. We KNOW the antidote to send this virus back to the pits of hell where it emerged, and where it must die. The antidote is alive and well; His name is Jesus. The power to heal lies within us. God is faithful to answer our prayers if we only believe.

Study Your Scripture:

Jeremiah 8: 21-22, NIV

"Since my people are crushed, I am crushed; I mourn, and horror grips me. Is there no balm in Gilead? Is there no physician there? Why then is there no healing for the wound of my people?"

Sing Your Song:

"Healing" by Richard Smallwood

Tell Your Tale:

Is there anything in your life causing worry or strife? How has your world been disrupted? What have you hung on to for endurance during hard times?

_____
_____
_____
_____
_____
_____
_____
_____
_____
_____
_____
_____
_____
_____
_____
_____
_____
_____

Activate The Antidote

Hope is a word often heard in a Christian environment. Hope offers an option when there seems to be few. Hope and faith go together, like peas and carrots. Although they are okay alone, together they make a powerful statement. In the unease and uncertainty of your daily plans, do you have hope?

When we feel we do not have hope, be reminded that our hope is in Christ and Him alone. We do not have to suffer with no end in sight. While we sit in our homes, feet apart from our loved ones, there is plenty of time, room, and opportunity to call on the Lord. God, on His throne, saw the direction in which we were heading. He saw people mocking the disabled, leaving the widowed to fend for themselves. He saw people hungry and homeless, yet they were not given food or shelter. He saw selfish living and reckless decision making. He saw His people knowingly defy His commands and turn their back on Him. He watched our demise with disappointment and disdain. So now, He has stilled our world so that we can concentrate on Him for help. Lord knows we need it!

Your second opportunity is here. It is such a blessing that we serve a God of many chances. You are His; He has claimed you as His own. So, humble yourself. Come down off your high horse and pray. Get on your knees and turn from your wicked ways. Stay in submission and prayer until you see Him. Until you hear from Him. Until a change comes this way. GOD promises us that if we do as He said, He will hear us, He will forgive us, and He will heal us in this present land. We need healing right now. Let's activate our anointing so we can receive the antidote from above.

Study Your Scripture:

2 Chronicles 7: 13-16, NIV

"When I shut up the heavens so that there is no rain, or command locusts to devour the land or send a plague among my people, if my people, who are called by my name, will humble themselves and pray and seek my face and turn from their wicked ways, then I will hear from heaven, and I will forgive their sin and will heal their land. Now my eyes will be open and my ears attentive to the prayers offered in this place. I have chosen and consecrated this temple so that my Name may be there forever. My eyes and my heart will always be there."

Sing Your Song:

"Spirit Fall Down" by Luther Barnes and The Red Budd Gospel Choir

Tell Your Tale:

Clearly, prayer is what we need for every situation. What do you need from God today? Share your earnest plea with Him below.

_____

_____

_____

_____

_____

_____

_____

_____

_____

_____

_____

_____

_____

_____

_____

_____

_____

_____

_____

Dear Lord,

We are living in a horror story right now. It appears that there is no right answer, no cure, no sure-fire preventative way to stop this illness called Covid-19 from attacking our bodies and wrecking our very existence. It looks like this plague wants to wipe us out. Lord, we know that it is not You or of You. But only You have the power to stop the enemy's plan right now. We cast out his evil scheme and call on Your mighty hand to direct the doctors, lead the scientist, heal the patients, and calm the anxious. We call on You to show the enemy, disguised as a ferocious virus, who You truly are. Lord, we turn away from all wrongdoing, backbiting, lying, and ugly ways. We know our ways don't always lead to You, but the path You have paved is open and ready if we so choose to follow. We are ready, Lord, to obey. We need You

to heal our land. In You, oh Lord, we have our only

HOPE.

In Jesus' name, Amen.

Songs of Comfort

He's Able

Do you truly believe that God is able? Although I know that He can do more than we could ever think of, I've found myself in situations searching for the right words to help someone else. What words can bring comfort in difficult situations such as a divorce, a traumatic loss, a wayward child, a negative medical diagnosis, or just a difficult day? Everything that we need to provide comfort to others is in the Word of God.

God revealed himself as El Shaddai—God Almighty in the Old Testament. He is the same today as He was then. He is never changing and forever faithful. He can do whatever He wants whenever He wants. He is strong, mighty, and all power is His. God wants you to lean on Him and trust Him with all your being. He knows that we are not able to conceptualize His power and majesty; however, He asked that rhetorical question in Genesis, "Is anything too hard for me?" It was not too much for God to form all creation, destroy lands, and rebuild again. He made kings out of shepherd boys and sent his LOVE in human form to save us from ourselves. Battles were won with a bow and arrow; chains were broken, and shackles released...all because He's able.

God is not a God that He should lie, and His Word is filled with His promises. God promised us that He would fight our battles. He promised that He would go before us, with us and never leave us. He promised to give us peace. He promised to renew our strength. He's willing and He's ABLE. Jesus left us with these words, "Ask in my name, and it shall be done." I challenge you to do just that today—ask, believe, and watch it happen. He's able!

Study Your Scripture:

Ephesians 3:14-21, NIV

"For this reason I kneel before the Father, from whom every family in heaven and on earth derives its name. I pray that out of his glorious riches he may strengthen you with power through his Spirit in your inner being, so that Christ may dwell in your hearts through faith. And I pray that you, being rooted and established in love, may have power, together with all the Lord's holy people, to grasp how wide and long and high and deep is the love of Christ, and to know this love that surpasses knowledge—that you may be filled to the measure of all the fullness of God. Now to him who is able to do immeasurably more than all we ask or imagine, according to his power that is at work within us, to him be glory in the church and in Christ Jesus throughout all generations, forever and ever! Amen."

Sing Your Song:

"He's Able" by Dietrick Haddon

Tell Your Tale:

What have you been able to accomplish because of God's favor in your life?

_____

_____

_____

_____

_____

_____

_____

_____

_____

_____

_____

_____

_____

_____

_____

_____

_____

_____

Hidden in Plain Sight

You cannot hide from trouble. It will have you crying and lying. It can leave you in a state of constant distress. Trouble will have your nerves shot, especially if you do not turn to God for help. Throughout my parenting journey, I had to call on God many times for direction and protection for my child. As a youngster, my sweet girl was no stranger to trouble. It always seemed to be in her way. Sometimes it was her fault. Most times, it was not.

Nevertheless, when trouble came, calling on the name of Jesus was always the first line of defense. My family called on God and asked Him to hide her so that she could not be found in trouble. We asked Him to elevate her so that no harm could touch her frame.

So, the story goes, when my daughter was in elementary school, I hated to receive a call from her school. Whenever those digits would appear, I would take a deep breath and begin to prepare myself for what lay ahead. Most times, the call was simply a reminder that a paper was due, a medication refill was needed, or that my child was absent or tardy. However, when that phone rang, my mind immediately thought of trouble. It could be in the form of an office referral, an asthma attack, or a lack of funds for lunch. As a parent, I wanted to protect my child from all hurt, harm, or danger. If she caused the trouble, she deserved the consequence. But if she was in trouble because of the enemy's evil ways, she needed

God's supernatural power to help her. And God did more than I could ever imagine on her behalf. He hid her in the time of trouble. He placed people in her life who would love her just for her. He hid her behind strong women of God, who prayed for her and taught her. He hid her in the hearts of teachers, administrators, daycare workers, and close family friends. He hid her in His pavilion, which was His covering. He hid her in His tabernacle, which was her school of learning.

God desires for us to seek him in times of distress. He wants to show us His thoughts, His love, and His way. When the time is right, He will set us up on a rock. Although trouble may come, trouble will not prevail. The devil's schemes are no match for God's covering. Tell your "trouble" to find a new place to play because you are carefully hidden in plain sight. You are covered, sheltered, and protected in the bosom of God. Get comfortable; you're safe.

Study Your Scripture:

Psalm 27: 1-5, NIV

"The Lord is my light and my salvation whom shall I fear? The Lord is the stronghold of my life of whom shall I be afraid. When the wicked advance against me to devour me, it is my enemies and my foes who will stumble and fall. Though an army besiege me, my heart will not fear, though war break out against me, even then I will be confident. One thing I ask from the Lord, this only do I seek, that I may dwell in the house of the Lord all the days of my life, to gaze on the

beauty of the Lord and to seek him in his temple.

For in the day of trouble he will keep me safe in

his dwelling; he will hide me in the shelter of his

sacred tent and set me high upon a rock."

Sing Your Song:

"A Secret Place" by Karen Clark Sheard

Tell Your Tale:

Describe your daily prayer routine. If you were able to design your perfect "secret place," how would it look? What tools would you need to connect with God?

_____

_____

_____

_____

_____

_____

_____

_____

_____

_____

_____

_____

_____

_____

_____

_____

Never Alone, No, Never Alone

Did you know that when you go through terrible times, you're never alone? I've had many moments of despair, hurt, pain, restless nights, disturbing phone calls, and numerous attacks from the enemy. It seemed like friends turned away from me, and my support system was crumbling on every side. My words were misconstrued and distorted. Lonely but not alone, sad but unable to describe why. Depression reared its ugly head, and anxiety held me captive in my own home.

At that time, it was so easy to complain. When you are mentally in a bad headspace, the appearance of everything around you is bad as well. It may seem that your workplace is miserable, your family responsibilities have become more of a burden than a blessing, and there is no exit from that desperate, deep dark hole, but God. My first reaction was to seek comfort from my mama, my sister, or a best friend. I wanted their comfort and assurance that I would make it through this difficult season. Although I tried, I couldn't find the words to ask for help. There were so many emotions but so few words; therefore, the travail was mine alone. Refusing to allow my few and simple words to fall on ears that could only hear but held no power to heal or reveal, I concealed my pain from man and prayed quietly to the Lord above. I needed my savior and big brother, Jesus, to intercede on my behalf. I needed Him to interpret my cries, unpack my groans, and release my wails. Jesus wept with me and God heard my cry. For so long, I felt no one could understand the inner turmoil that plagued my very spirit. But God kept me, never left me, walked with me, and protected me. He's willing, ready, and able to do the same for you. He heard me, and He will hear you too. In your deepest valley, find comfort in knowing that you are never alone.

Study Your Scripture:

Job 7: 16-19, NIV

"I despise my life; I would not live forever. Let me alone; my days have no meaning. What is mankind that you make so much of them, that you give them so much attention, that you examine them every morning and test them every moment. Will you never look away from me, or let me be alone even for an instant?"

Deuteronomy 31:6, NIV

"Be strong and courageous. Do not be afraid or terrified because of them, for the Lord your God goes with you; he will never leave you nor forsake you."

Sing Your Song:

"I Almost Let Go" by Kurt Carr

Tell Your Tale:

Who do you seek out first in difficult times? It's important to have God close by in "valley situations." What activities do you intentionally perform to deepen your relationship with God?

_____
_____
_____
_____
_____
_____
_____
_____
_____
_____
_____
_____
_____
_____
_____
_____
_____
_____

Looking Good While Going Through

Why is that during some of the bleakest times in life, people tend to see and compliment your "glow up" but are unable to notice what you had to endure just to "show up?" In my deepest valleys, I did not have a physical hand to steady me, guide me, or help me. However, each day, to the best of my ability, I put on my best dress, my eyeshadow and lipstick and tried to give the world my very best. Although broken inside, I received compliments such as "Get it, sis," "Go girl," and "You're living your best life." Although thankful, I grew weary of hearing these phrases. Not because I was conceited, instead, it was quite the opposite. I did not feel I deserved those praises, nor did I think that it was true of my current situation. I wanted to be transparent and shout to all who would hear, "Hey, I don't have it together. Everything is falling apart. I'm hurting. I'm aching. I'm fighting demonic spirits left and right." I wanted to complain. But God bridled my tongue, and out of my obedience, His words were edified. God still got the praise!

Sisters/brothers, we are not immune to life circumstances. They touch us all from time to time, some more so than others, but victory is on the other side of the pressing. Your pressing does not have to look like disheveled hair and untidy clothing. It does not have to be filled with complaint after complaint. It does not have to be numbed with drugs and alcohol. It does not have to be concealed in an insane mind with no direction and no hope. Friends thought they saw ME shining, but what they saw was God beaming through me. They saw God illuminating His love and His light for others to see. Yield not to complaints, for better days are coming. You do not have to suffer alone or look bad in times of distress. Call out to God, and press your way through. Take it from me; you can look good while doing it!

Study Your Scripture:

Philippians 3:12-21, NIV

"Not that I have already obtained all this, or have already arrived at my goal, but I press on to take hold of that for which Christ Jesus took hold of me.

Brothers and sisters, I do not consider myself yet to have taken hold of it. But one thing I do: Forgetting what is behind and straining toward what is ahead, I press on toward the goal to win the prize for which God has called me heavenward in Christ Jesus. All of us, then, who are mature should take such a view of things. And if on some point you think differently, that too God will make clear to you. Only let us live up to what we have already attained. Join together in following my example, brothers and sisters, and just as you have us as a model, keep your eyes on those who live as we do. For, as I have often told you before and now tell you again even with tears, many live as enemies of the cross of Christ. Their destiny is destruction, their god is their stomach, and their glory is in their shame. Their mind is set on earthly things. But our citizenship is in heaven. And we eagerly await a Savior from there, the Lord Jesus Christ, who, by the power that enables him to bring everything under his control, will transform our lowly bodies so that they will be like his glorious body."

Sing Your Song:

"Press My Way Through" by Bishop Paul Morton

Tell Your Tale:

How do you handle difficult times? Is it easier to complain or to seek the good in the situation? Why or why not? Describe a situation where you have pressed through.

_____
_____
_____
_____
_____
_____
_____
_____
_____
_____
_____
_____
_____
_____
_____
_____

Pack Light

As you prepare for the day's travels, pack light. Give God all those things that make you heavy, for they will only slow you down and make you tired...and weak...and bothered. Don't start the new day carrying yesterday's troubles. God will give you rest from all the heartaches, worries, and scars from the past, but you must let it go. It's too much for you to tote along the way.

Imagine this. Cheers to the ultimate girl trip! For over a year, my girls and I had been planning to travel out of the country together. The time drew near, and I'd been packing daily for a week. My clothes and shoes were spilling out of my suitcase. However hard I tried, everything wouldn't fit inside. I wanted to downsize but I needed an outfit for every possible event, two pairs of shoes for every outfit, and three sets of jewelry for every pair of shoes. Whew, I know it seems like a lot, but this self-proclaimed "girly girl" wanted to be prepared. After days of packing, unpacking, and packing again, finally, my suitcase closed (barely) and I was ready to roll. With smiles all around, I happily placed my suitcase on the airport's scale to check my bags. What should have been a simple process suddenly became complicated and scary. Lights began to flash around, and the sirens started to sound. Suddenly, an attendant came from behind and shouted out to me, "Your bags are too heavy. You must lighten your load." As I frantically began to shift items, discard extras, and reorganize the excess, another voice softly stated, "Ma'am, I can see that you are burdened by this sudden change of plans. You do not need to stress. You can carry all of your things with you, but you have to pay an extra fee." With deep breaths of relief, I began to gather my change and count my pennies to cover the cost, and yet another voice spoke to me. This voice was different, yet familiar, and it said to me, *"You cannot carry your new blessings while holding on to your old burdens."* It was the voice of God telling me to let...it...go.

There comes a time when we must discard those people, things, and thoughts that weigh us down. They are the "heavyweight" which makes getting to the next destination an arduous task. I am confident that God has something big for you up ahead, but you need room to carry it to your next destination. Drop off the excess weight so you don't have to pay the fee of being burdened or being a burden to others. Lighten your load today.

Study Your Scripture:

Matthew 11: 28-30, NIV

"Come to me, all you who are weary and burdened, and I will give you rest. Take my yoke upon you and learn from me, for I am gentle and humble in heart, and you will find rest for your souls. For my yoke is easy and my burden is light."

Sing Your Song:

"I Surrender All" by Israel Houghton

Tell Your Tale:

What's in your bag that you need to let go? What can you give to God to make your load a little lighter?

_____

_____

_____

_____

_____

_____

_____

_____

_____

_____

_____

_____

_____

_____

_____

_____

_____

Dear Lord,

Today's bags are heavy, and I need to unpack before I close my eyes. I'm dropping off a few heavy items with You. Thanks in advance for lightening my load; they've been too heavy for me for way too long. So I leave my worries with You. Please give me peace to comfort me. I leave with You my unfinished business. I've dealt with what I can for the day, tomorrow will take care of itself. With the sunshine, I see new mercies. I leave with You my heartache. Please fill my heart with joy. Help me to rest up for I see many blessings ahead. I need strength. I cannot carry my new blessings bogged down with the weight of the old burdens. Those burdens You have asked for and those strongholds You have released me from, they're Yours. Take the pain and give me joy. Take the sleepless nights and give me rest. I'm so glad that Your yoke is easy, and Your burden is light. Most days my burden is heavy because my human nature likes to fight my spirit man at times. I'm stronger now, so at this moment, I place it all on You. Thank You, Lord, You've already picked up the load. I'm lighter, I'm better, and blessed to be called Your child. With comfort in my spirit and peace in my soul, I give all praise to You.

In Jesus' name, Amen.

Songs of Freedom

I Woke Up Like This

The popular adage "I woke up like this" became a sensation around the year of 2014. Perhaps it was a selfie in bed, or a fresh face with no makeup, or even hair sprawled all over the place taken to represent the pride women had in their natural state. At first, I was a fan. I loved the idea that women had finally become happy within themselves and had finally dismissed the mainstream idea of beauty, whatever that may be. Then slowly, the real insecurities swept in. The pictures changed and the filters evolved. The selfie in bed became staged with matching pajamas and sheets, the fresh face was altered with a "natural" makeup look. The hair was perfectly teased into a messy bun, maybe a little unkept but cute, nonetheless. Just as quickly as I became a fan, I was no longer. I desire for us to love who we are, the wrinkles, the moles, the crooked nose, and all. I'm convinced that God looks down at us every single morning, shakes His head, sighs, and whispers softly, "If you could only see what I see."

God's Word provides us with many truths of who we are and who we are called to be in His name. Why is it so hard for us to believe? Perhaps it's a problem with our hearing. Are you able to hear God's voice above others? Are you able to tune out those voices that scream hateful and self-loathing words? Are you willing to ignore the multitude of voices determined to create doubt in your beauty and in your abilities? God sees and tells us in a still quiet voice, "You are beautiful, just like you are. And really, my love, you woke up like this. Better yet, you were created like this. You were created in My image. Everything on you was crafted for you, and I love it. If you could only see what I see." There is nothing created on earth that He did not have a hand in or, better yet, handcraft Himself. Yes, that includes you. We were made fearfully and wonderfully, with Godly attributes of knowledge, love, and the ability to know Him fully. Your perceived flaws are instruments designed by God, so that He may do His good and perfect work, in you and through you, for others to see. You have a purpose, and it's so much more than a filtered selfie. You, my dear sister/brother, are perfectly imperfect just the way you were created to be!

Study Your Scripture:

Ephesians 2:1-9, NIV

"As for you, you were dead in your transgressions and sins, in which you used to live when you followed the ways of this world and of the ruler of the kingdom of the air, the spirit who is now at work in those who are disobedient. All of us also lived among them at one time, gratifying the cravings of our flesh and following its desires and thoughts. Like the rest, we were by nature deserving of wrath. But because of his great love for us, God, who is rich in mercy, made us alive with Christ even when we were dead in transgressions—it is by grace you have been saved. And God raised us up with Christ and seated us with him in the heavenly realms in Christ Jesus, in order that in the coming ages he might show the incomparable riches of his grace, expressed in his kindness to us in Christ Jesus. For it is by grace you have been saved, through faith— and this is not from yourselves, it is the gift of God—not by works, so that no one can boast. For we are God's handiwork, created in Christ Jesus to do good works, which God prepared in advance for us to do."

Psalm 139:14, NIV

"I praise you because I am fearfully and wonderfully made; your works are wonderful; I know that full well."

Revelation 4:11, NIV

"You are worthy, our Lord and God, to receive glory and honor and power, for you created all things, and by your will they were created and have their being."

Sing Your Song:

"He Still Loves Me" by Beyoncé and Walter Williams

Tell Your Tale:

List your favorite features. Are you comfortable with your natural God-given beauty? What routine do you regularly perform to enhance your inner and outer beauty?

_____
_____
_____
_____
_____
_____
_____
_____
_____
_____
_____
_____
_____
_____
_____
_____
_____

A Passionate Plea

"She's passionate!" Honestly, I've heard that description of me throughout my life, more times than I care to admit. I initially viewed it as an offensive statement. When I think of a passionate person, I envision a boisterous, intense, persistent know-it-all who prides themself on imposing their beliefs on others. It sounds sort of negative to me. But does it truly carry a negative connotation in the biblical sense? Is there a possibility that God desires more passion when seeking Him?

Several passages in the Bible demonstrate how God is faithful in responding to passionate pleas. We've heard the story about the woman who dealt with the issue of blood for twelve long years before she was able to be healed. Although her detailed story is not recorded, I imagine that she prayed for healing of the unbearable cramps, the uncontrollable flow, and the restless nights that tormented her body. It's likely that she sought the opinions of medical experts, attempted home remedies, and pleaded to God for healing. To many, it may have looked as if the woman sought Jesus out as a last-ditch effort. I'm more inclined to believe that she knew the answer was with Jesus alone. She was passionate in her effort to reach the true healer. Just before all of this took place, a synagogue leader approached Jesus and passionately pleaded for His assistance as well. Sounds familiar, right? Everyone always calls on Jesus at the same time. Isn't it ironic how He responds to the passionate pleas immediately! Although few words were shared by the followers, the words were spoken with such a passionate assurance in the power of Jesus. The leader said, "My daughter is dead, but I need you to touch her so that she will live." That request is humanly impossible. Can you imagine how foolish this man looked to others? However, God answered his plea. Who can ignore those types of pleas?

The impossible occurs, when passion, purpose, and God's plan meet. God responds to our unfailing and passionate belief! Jesus responds positively to passionate cries for help. He wants you to seek Him with a boisterous voice, an intense desire, a persistent cry, and a know-it-all mindset that He can do all things.   Passion pleases the Father!

Study Your Scripture:

Matthew 9: 18-26, NIV

"While he was saying this, a synagogue leader came and knelt before him and said, "My daughter has just died. But come and put your hand on her, and she will live." Jesus got up and went with him, and so did his disciples. Just then, a woman who had been subject to bleeding for twelve years came up behind him and touched the edge of his cloak. She said to herself, "If I only touch his cloak, I will be healed." Jesus turned and saw her. "Take heart, daughter," he said, "your faith has healed you." And the woman was healed at that moment. When Jesus entered the synagogue leader's house and saw the noisy crowd and people playing pipes, he said, "Go away. The girl is not dead but asleep." But they laughed at him. After the crowd had been put outside, he went in and took the girl by the hand, and she got up. News of this spread through all that region."

Sing Your Song:

"A Little More Jesus" by Erica Campbell

Tell Your Tale:

What are you willing to fight for with all your might? In what venture, person, or activity does your passion flow?

_____

_____

_____

_____

_____

_____

_____

_____

_____

_____

_____

_____

_____

_____

_____

_____

_____

Who's the Boss?

You, nor do I, get to tell God what to do, how to do it, or when to do it. This truth was hard for me to accept. It may be difficult for you as well; however, it is a truth, nonetheless. I know that you're in a hurry for your next big break, promotion, graduation, husband, luxury car, perfect body, or miracle child. Unfortunately, it is not in your hands. Albeit better, it's in the hands of God, who knows what's best for you. God decides *if* we will obtain our heart's desire and *when* we shall receive that blessing. He does all things in His perfect timing. I've cried out to God and given instructions on how I would like my life to go, yet I am still waiting for my plans to evolve as I expected. I've come to accept that my plans may never come to fruition. I've learned to give up some control, and now I choose to "BOSS" up in this way.

B-Be

O-Obedient and

S-Stay

S-Still while God directs my path.

I'm sure you are familiar with the story of Job. The devil attacked him and despite Job's pain and loss, he worshipped God. Until one day, he forgot who the boss was and questioned the Big Man above. He cried out to the Lord with frustration and angst. After a waiting period, God responded. It was probably not the response that

Job was expecting. God inquired about Job's existence when He set heaven and earth in place and created all the land and sea. Job was given the task of stating how many stars were in the sky, and to provide the measurements from east to west and from night until day. Just as we can be, like a stubborn child, Job attempted a rebuttal. Again, he was silenced. Eventually, Job decided to BOSS up (Be Obedient and Stay Still). Job confessed his weakness and gave God all the praise. At that time, God gave Job more than he could have ever asked or dreamed of and gave him double for his trouble. Through Job's prayers, his friends were forgiven and blessed. Talk about a BOSS move. God's plans are always bigger and better than what you, or I, could ever imagine.

Study Your Scripture:

Job 42, NIV

"Then Job replied to the Lord "I know that you can do all things; no purpose of yours can be thwarted. You asked, 'Who is this that obscures my plans without knowledge?' Surely, I spoke of things I did not understand, things too wonderful for me to know. "You said, 'Listen now, and I will speak, I will question you, and you shall answer me.' My ears had heard of you but now my eyes have seen you. Therefore, I despise myself and repent in dust and ashes." After the Lord had said these things to Job, he said to Eliphaz the Temanite, "I am angry with you and your two friends, because you have not spoken the truth about me, as my servant Job has. So now take seven bulls and seven rams and go to my servant Job and sacrifice a burnt offering for yourselves. My servant Job will pray for you, and I will accept his prayer and not deal with you according to your folly. You have not spoken the truth about me, as my servant Job has." So Eliphaz the Temanite, Bildad the Shuhite and Zophar the Naamathite did what the Lord told them; and the Lord accepted Job's prayer. After Job had prayed for his friends, the Lord restored his fortunes and gave him twice as much as he had before. All his brothers and sisters and everyone who had known him before came and ate with him in his house. They comforted and consoled him over all the trouble the Lord had brought on him, and each one gave him a piece of silver and a gold ring. The Lord blessed the latter part of Job's life more than the former part. He had fourteen thousand sheep, six thousand camels, a thousand yoke of oxen and a thousand donkeys. And he also had seven sons and three daughters. The first daughter he named Jemimah, the second Keziah and the third Keren-Happuch. Nowhere in all the land were there found women as beautiful as Job's daughters, and their father granted them an inheritance along with their brothers. After this, Job lived a hundred and forty years; he saw his children and their children to the fourth generation. And so Job died, an old man and full of years."

Sing Your Song:

"The Lord is the Boss" by Dillon Loving

Tell Your Tale:

What have you "told" God that you "need" Him to do? How has He humbled you in your asking and your expectations?

_____
_____
_____
_____
_____
_____
_____
_____
_____
_____
_____
_____
_____
_____
_____
_____
_____
_____
_____

Salty and Lit

Just call me Ms. Salty and Lit. The Urban Dictionary defines salty as "the act of being upset, angry, or bitter as a result of being made fun of or embarrassed." Likewise, the word lit is defined as being "high" or having an experience of something that is "fun and exciting." Who knew? What would you think if I proudly told you that's how all of us should desire to be seen? Honestly, I believe that it's true. After assiduously studying God's word, I received a revelation on this popular phrase. Those words can have a bigger and greater meaning in life. One that, if represented with precision and purpose, could season a people with God's word and light a city with just a small flame. How awesome would it be if you could be "Salty and Lit" for God?

If you woke up today unsure of your mission or specific purpose, know this, you are called to be the salt of the earth. You are to sprinkle the fruit of the spirit wherever you go. Be sure to leave a little goodness, a dash of kindness, a splatter of joy, a speckle of peace, a fleck of patience, a heaping cup of love, a dapple of self-control, and dots of faithfulness behind. Season your covered ground well. A little "seasoning" will go a long way. People will then want more of what you are serving; they will want more of God.

As for your sparkle, you are designed for the bright lights! A light is not meant to be hidden. Do not let others dull your shine or see you as too much of anything. You can never be too extra, too holy, or too bright. As a child of God, you are elevated. You are called to be set apart. The light emitted from you is magnified to shed light on the one above, your Savior, your Maker, your Creator, your Redeemer, the one and only living God. Let your light shine so that others can see God and give Him glory. Shine bright, my sister/brother. Stay a little salty; it's what you were made for. "Salty and Lit," sprinkling, and shining...for God.

Study Your Scripture:

Matthew 5: 13-16, NIV

"You are the salt of the earth. But if the salt loses its saltiness, how can it be made salty again? It is no longer good for anything, except to be thrown out and trampled underfoot. "You are the light of the world. A town built on a hill cannot be hidden. Neither do people light a lamp and put it under a bowl. Instead they put it on its stand, and it gives light to everyone in the house. In the same way, let your light shine before others, that they may see your good deeds and glorify your Father in heaven."

Sing Your Song:

"You Brought the Sunshine" by The Clark Sisters

Tell Your Tale:

This passage referenced the fruit of the spirit. See if you can list them below. Which fruit of the spirit do you already bear? Which fruit are you trying to grow? (For more information on the fruit of the spirit, read Galatians 5:22-23.)

_____

_____

_____

_____

_____

_____

_____

_____

_____

_____

_____

_____

_____

_____

_____

_____

_____

Give It Up to God

As a professional social worker, my job involves interacting with people from all walks of life. I have the privilege of working with the most affluent, the disenfranchised, the hurt, the hopeless, the successful, and the underachievers. I've shared laughs, experienced hurts, and even assisted in diverting some horrible situations. I've empathized with some and even pitied a few. The torturous trials people have faced and the obstacles they have overcome just to survive from day to day are astounding and quite unimaginable. More often than not, I meet people at their worst. But after talking with them, it's often easy to see that they are actually operating at their absolute personal best for that day. They've sought out help despite what their family may have said or thought. They've set aside embarrassment and guilt in order to share their inner secrets with me. Although attentive and concerned on the exterior, the inside of my heart is often full, at the point of combustion. Their pain, their anguish, their memories, their scars overwhelm me. Sometimes, I just want to give up.

Give up on this profession

Give up on expectations

Give up on my calling

Give up on hope

Give up on humanity

Give up on education

Give up on the justice system

Give up on the potential that I see in others

And even in myself

So, I did. I gave "it" up to God. All negativity, all insecurities, all misunderstandings, all ailments, all situations, I gave it to Him. I gave up on my ability to have all the right answers and to offer the instant fix. Only He who can do all things but fail is able to handle this heavy stuff. I know from experience that He will be waiting to receive and relieve all of your troubles. This experience was freeing. We are not able to do our best work unless we allow God to work in us and through us. Free yourself from the responsibility of doing it all. Give it all to God and watch Him work it out!

Study Your Scripture:

Philippians 4:13, NIV

"I can do all this through him who gives me strength."

Psalm 5:22, NIV

"Cast your cares on the Lord and he will sustain you. He will never let the righteous be shaken."

Deuteronomy 15:10, NIV

"Give generously to them and do so without a grudging heart; then because of this the Lord your God will bless you in all your work and in everything you put your hand to. "

Sing Your Song:

"I Give Myself Away" by William McDowell

Tell Your Tale:

Reflect on a time that you had to free yourself from something holding you back. What was it? How did you know you were overloaded and overwhelmed? How did God relieve those troubles?

_____
_____
_____
_____
_____
_____
_____
_____
_____
_____
_____
_____
_____
_____
_____
_____
_____

Dear Father God,

I need Your holy word to fill my heart and mind. I need to be reminded of who I am in You. I feel bound by life's circumstances. I feel that there are chains holding me back from doing what You would have me to do. Remove this muzzle from my mouth which tries to prevent me from speaking Your truth and sharing Your word. Lord, I need You to free me from this overwhelming pressure to be perfect before I speak about Your goodness. Free me from the expectation to always do right before I try to lead someone in Your direction. Remind me of the freedom that I received when Jesus died on the cross. Thank you, Lord. He freed me! He freed me from uncertain death. He freed me from the commandments that I've failed to keep. He freed me from perfectionism. There is none perfect but You, oh God. Through Jesus' obedience and sacrifice, my freedom has come. Whom the Son sets free is free indeed. Thank You, Lord, that I can live unfiltered for You. Thank You, Lord, that I can be salty and lit and a Christian too. Thank You, Lord, that I've been set free. Thank you, Lord, that my mind is unlocked, and my soul is free in You.

In the matchless name of Christ, Amen.

Sounds of

Victory

Praising God for the Victory

School's out! All the kids were ready to shout! The time had come for the official kickoff of summertime, Vacation Bible School (VBS). Every June, families planned their vacations around the most popular VBS sites, just so their kids could attend. At VBS, we played with friends, laughed about fun times, learned pledges to the Christian flag and the Bible, heard classic Bible stories, created handcrafted treasures, played foursquare and hopscotch. And as a final treat, we were given a snack bag of sweet butter cookies and red juice. Hmm, hmm good and such good memories! However, my most precious memory is when all the VBS participants, young and old, would gather in the sanctuary to sing the song, Father Abraham. Good ole Father Abraham was an interactive piece. In order to sing it correctly, we had to move our arms, stomp our feet, turn around, jump up and down, then finally sit down. That song wore us out! I never understood the purpose of the movements...until now.

During Abraham's time, the Jewish people were under the law. Step by step, they were given instruction as a way to bring them closer to the Savior, yet they failed miserably. At one point, Abraham was asked to sacrifice his son, Isaac. Although this task was difficult, Abraham trusted in God to provide a way. Can you imagine the sweat dripping from Abraham's brow or the tremor in his voice as he spoke to Isaac? He was physically tired from climbing the hill and mentally exhausted from worrying about the outcome. Just as Abraham was at the place of giving out, God offered him another alternative, a ram in the bush. Hallelujah! After Abraham gave his all, God gave even more.

Here's the note for us: all of that moving that Abraham did was good and dandy, but what made the difference in his situation was his belief in God. Once Abraham saw his way out, he gave God praise, such as the purpose of the movements in the VBS song that I loved as a child. After swinging our arms, screaming to the high heavens, stretching our bodies from side to side, we finally had to sit down, hear, and BELIEVE in God's Word. You see, faith and hard work go together. One lesson that VBS taught me is we can work hard at something, but eventually we must sit down, trust God, and give Him the praise!

Study Your Scripture:

Galatians 3:5-14, NIV

"So again I ask, does God give you his Spirit and work miracles among you by the works of the law, or by your believing what you heard? So also Abraham "believed God, and it was credited to him as righteousness." Understand, then, that those who have faith are children of Abraham. Scripture foresaw that God would justify the Gentiles by faith, and announced the gospel in advance to Abraham: "All nations will be blessed through you." So those who rely on faith are blessed along with Abraham, the man of faith. For all who rely on the works of the law are under a curse, as it is written: "Cursed is everyone who does not continue to do everything written in the Book of the Law." Clearly no one who relies on the law is justified before God, because "the righteous will live by faith." The law is not based on faith; on the contrary, it says, "The person who does these things will live by them." Christ redeemed us from the curse of the law by becoming a curse for us, for it is written: "Cursed is everyone who is hung on a pole." He redeemed us in order that the blessing given to Abraham might come to the Gentiles through Christ Jesus, so that by faith we might receive the promise of the Spirit."

Sing Your Song:

"Father Abraham" by Unknown

Tell Your Tale:

Describe a time that God asked you to move outside of your traditional comfort zone. What uncomfortable moves did you make to achieve the goal?

_____
_____
_____
_____
_____
_____
_____
_____
_____
_____
_____
_____
_____
_____
_____
_____

Run the Race That Was Meant for You

Ready, set, go. What race are you running through life? Is it a race to be the most popular? Is it a race to be the most successful? Is it a race against your competition, or is it the race to get to the other side? Whatever your race is, just make sure you are running the race that's meant for you. Your purposed journey may take you to a different route than the world has outlined. Be assured that *if* you are on the right path and pursuing the journey proposed for you, you will arrive at the destination that God has for you.

When I think of a race, I imagine a mass of people at the start line. They are prepared with running gear (salts, water, energy bars, and a fanny pack) and sporting their most broken-in but favorite running shoes. Some runners may present with matching shirts and cute tutus. Nevertheless, everyone is bubbling over with excitement and raring to take off. We may never know the reason each runner chose to participate in a specific race. Maybe they joined the race to support a specific cause or because they are an avid runner and love to hail as the champion in their age category. Maybe they have been training all year for this very moment, or maybe they want to knock an item off their bucket list, as they have been handed a diagnosis with a grim prognosis. Just as the reasons for starting the journey (race) varies, so will the experiences and the end results. Although they may be tired, sweaty, and plain ole exhausted; ultimately, the goal is to see each runner at the finish line.

At the end of your journey or race, there will be just one winner. You may start with many others, but remember you are not running the same race. Rest assured, when you cross the finish line, there will be a host of people congratulating you on your journey. People have been watching you from afar and rooting in the background. They will be there to greet you just as there will be a host of angels welcoming you into the heavenly gates when that time comes. Not one person will be focused on the one who hit the finish line first. At that final moment, it will be all about you. You would've won the race that was intended for you. Glory! Keep running towards your destiny.

Study Your Scripture:

1 Corinthians 9:24-27, NIV

"Do you not know that in a race all the runners run, but only one gets the prize? Run in such a way as to get the prize. Everyone who competes in the games goes into strict training. They do it to get a crown that will not last, but we do it to get a crown that will last forever. Therefore I do not run like someone running aimlessly; I do not fight like a boxer beating the air. No, I strike a blow to my body and make it my slave so that after I have preached to others, I will not be disqualified for the prize."

Sing Your Song:

"Running for Jesus" by Galilee Baptist Church
Mass Choir

Tell Your Tale:

Have you ever participated in a 5k or 10k race?
What motivated you to sign up? How did you
train for the race? If you compared your Christian
journey to a race, what steps are you taking to
make it to the finish line?

_____

_____

_____

_____

_____

_____

_____

_____

_____

_____

_____

_____

_____

_____

_____

Speak Pleasing Words

What if each time we opened our mouths, we sought out God first? Would our conversations sound differently? Would they be filtered with more grace and less judgment? Would the words be sweet and comforting? Would we always have the right words to say? Would we know when to speak and when to be quiet? A wordsmith may encompass extensive knowledge of the English language. Intelligence is knowing what to say. Quite the opposite, wisdom is knowing when to say it. The gift of wisdom is delivered from God above. Our heavenly Father will fashion our hearts, so our mouths speak of His goodness in every situation.

Out of the heart, the mouth speaks.   It is impossible to hide an evil heart. The mouth will tell it every time. It may be presented with a sly, sarcastic, shady comment, or maybe in an offhand compliment. Either way, if God is not in you, it will show. If He lives within you, He will show out through you, and others will be blessed.

How do we ensure our words are pure and clean? Our hearts must first be cleansed. We must receive a daily cleanse from the inside in order to speak in acceptance and accordance to God's will. We don't typically bathe once a week. We wash our bodies daily because of the dirt and filth that we come into contact throughout the day. Living in this sinful world, our hearts are exposed to dirt, filth, deceit, lies, and all kinds of debris. We must cleanse our hearts by asking God to let our words be acceptable and to make our hearts like His. Is this an easy task? It is not; however, it is a necessary task for us to speak pleasing words. Just as we make it a priority to take care of our outer body, we need to prioritize the care of our inner body, starting with our hearts and our minds. If our minds truly stay on God and the meditation of our hearts focus solely on Him, loving words will flow from our lips to the hearts of others. Feed your soul with God's goodness and watch your words so that they speak life to difficult circumstances. Be the good in your life and in others too.

Study Your Scripture:

Psalm 19:4, NIV

"May these words of my mouth and this meditation of my heart be pleasing in your sight, Lord, my Rock, and my Redeemer.

Sing Your Song:

"Grateful" by Hezekiah Walker

Tell Your Tale:

When one is upset, disgruntled, or hurt, it is easy
to say harsh and hurtful words. How do you
control your tongue in times of anger?

_____
_____
_____
_____
_____
_____
_____
_____
_____
_____
_____
_____
_____
_____
_____
_____
_____
_____

Are you Just Living or Are you Thriving?

What is driving you to fight against "no" and to take detours against rejection? Is your main desire to live from day to day? That's called the hustle. Or do you desire to thrive and achieve more than your wildest dreams? That's called passion and purpose. Which of these lifestyles sounds more pleasing to you? Ideally, our passion should drive us to fulfill our God-ordained purpose. The hustle, alone, is not going to give us the victory. It's important to be reminded that God yields to our beckoning call. Yes, we will have to do the leg work and build the muscle, but God provides the increase.

Everybody wants to be a hustler. It appears that today, the word hustler is a badge of honor and a source of pride. If someone is making money by excelling in their job or trade, others may refer to them as a hustler. And because of pop-culture, they are proud of it. However, the Merriam-Webster Dictionary defines the term as that of a person who is "making money in an illegal way or by fraud." It seems like we have it all wrong. Hustling is what the people "of the world" do. We are not hustlers; indeed, we are soldiers in God's army.

As Christians, we are workers in the vineyard. There is much work to do, and very few to do it. So yes, we work and we work hard. By surrendering to Christ's plan, we are guaranteed to have life and to have life more abundantly. The hustle that makes things happen comes from your will to please God and fulfill His purpose and plan for your life. The passion and the understanding that He who began a good work in you will complete it will guide you towards success. God's provision, protection, and direction will propel you forward despite any circumstances. Passion and purpose, desire, and design will always produce the best results. The hustle can change from day to day, but your passion and purpose should be firmly rooted in your desire to serve God. Are we just living and surviving or are we living and thriving for God?

Study Your Scripture:

John 10:10, NIV

"The thief comes only to steal and kill and destroy; I have come that they may have **life** and have it to the full."

Ephesians 3:14-21

"For this reason I kneel before the Father, from whom every family in heaven and on earth derives its name. I pray that out of his glorious riches, he may strengthen you with power through his Spirit in your inner being, so that Christ may dwell in your hearts through faith. And I pray that you, being rooted and established in love, may have power, together with all the Lord's holy people, to grasp how wide and long and high and deep is the love of Christ, and to know this love that surpasses knowledge—that you may be filled to the measure of all the fullness of God. Now to him who is able to do immeasurably more than all we ask or imagine, according to his power that is at work within us, to him be glory in the church and in Christ Jesus throughout all generations, forever and ever! Amen.

Sing Your Song:

"Is My Living in Vain" by The Clark Sisters

Tell Your Tale:

Passion drives your purpose. Describe your life's
purpose. What are you passionate about? Write
the steps needed to achieve your goals.

_____
_____
_____
_____
_____
_____
_____
_____
_____
_____
_____
_____
_____
_____
_____
_____
_____
_____

Victory Is In The Waiting

We want everything to happen fast, expediently, and without delay. Hold up! Let me tell you, waiting on the Lord has its benefits. When we move in our time, we may not have the strength to endure the strife and strain that often comes with success. God gives us what is needed from day to day. He assures us there is no need to worry about tomorrow, for He will provide, maintain, and protect us in the days to come. He will give us what is needed to do His will. In the waiting, in the wanting, and in the seeking we should be storing God's word to refuel our strength for the blessings to come. As a full night's sleep is needed to refuel, strength must be renewed each day. Depleting our daily dose of strength is expected, but GOD will renew and restore without delay.

After waiting, God's provision does not cease. He gives you the stance of an eagle. Bold, brave, courageous, and strong. An eagle flies without worry or concern. He soars. The eagle is propelled by what is behind, beneath, and beyond him. God gives us that kind of imperturbable confidence. Unfortunately, we will not soar forever. We will not always be at the top of our game. At some point, we must land. And in many cases, the landing may not be the expected destination. It may be breathtakingly beautiful, an illusion of paradise. But beyond the first glimpses of beauty, there may be murky mud and mire awaiting us. It is prophesied that we will run and not grow weary and walk and shall not faint.

Have you ever tried to run on the beach? The scenery is beautiful, the sand is sparkling, and the mirage of safety is present. However, just beyond the shore, danger may be lurking. God gives us the ability to run through the heavy mud, the quicksand, the rocks, and the shells placed strategically to slow us down. The truth is, that rugged trail may slow us down. So, walk if you may, but remember to keep moving because God has assured us that we will not faint. Oh, the benefits that we could reap if we could only learn to wait.

Study Your Scripture:

Isaiah 40:28-31, NIV

"Do you not know? Have you not heard? The Lord is the everlasting God, the Creator of the ends of the earth. He will not grow tired or weary, and his understanding no one can fathom. He gives strength to the weary and increases the power of the weak. Even youths grow tired and weary, and young men stumble and fall; but those who hope in the Lord will renew their strength. They will soar on wings like eagles; they will run and not grow weary, they will walk and not be faint."

Sing Your Song:

"I Don't Mind Waiting" by Juanita Bynum

Tell Your Tale:

What are the benefits of waiting on the Lord?
What have you prayed for that God, in His time,
delivered? Was it worth the wait?

_____

_____

_____

_____

_____

_____

_____

_____

_____

_____

_____

_____

_____

_____

_____

_____

_____

_____

Dear God,

I am passionate about fulfilling Your purpose. I know that my work is futile without Your direction. Remove the spirit of hustle from me, but fill me up with Your Holy Spirit. The Holy Spirit is a quiet but strong force to be reckoned with. Also, gentle but oh so, powerful. The Holy Spirit is a loyal partner and an excellent conductor. The Holy Spirit is Your presence, which was left to comfort me. The Holy Spirit feeds my passion and fuels my purpose.

My God, I am so driven to succeed but slow me down, if need be. I'm learning to wait on Your direction. In the waiting, I may become impatient but remind me that You have it all worked out for my good. I may need to be worked on a little while longer. Fix me, Lord, and make me more like You.

There is peace found in the period of waiting. There, I can hear Your voice without distraction. Thank You for continuing to pour more of You into me. I'll be right here waiting, dear God, until You tell me to move into my destiny.

In Jesus' name, Amen.

Songs of Love

Eternal Love

Have you ever played the "He loves me, He loves me not" game? If you never had the opportunity to play, you missed a crucial part of your childhood. Just kidding, well partially. The feeling that one would get from a simple game declaring that one is loved is indescribable. Whether young or old, love sparks a reaction, it is an electric charge that is needed to survive. But before I get ahead of myself, let's explore the rules of the game.

It's truly the easiest game one could play. First, you did not need a playmate to play. It was truly a game of one. You would close your eyes and concentrate on the name of a crush or a secret friend. You would say their name, with fingers crossed that they loved you as much as you loved them. Then, slowly you would begin to pluck the petals off the flower until you reached the very last petal. With each pluck, you would say the words, "He loves me" or "He loves me not." It was every little girl's dream that she would end up holding the last petal so that she could gleefully exclaim that "He loves me!" Now, it did not always play out like this. Sometimes the odds would not be in her favor. As she held that dreaded, "He loves me not" petal, her little heart would drop, and her lips would turn into an upside-down frown. The rejection would never last long, for she would quickly recover, choose another beautiful flower, and pluck away. This game would continue until her young self would be completely satisfied that she is indeed loved. Oh, how sweet it is to be loved!

As adults, we still desire to feel love. Sometimes we seek it in the wrong places and in the wrong relationships with the wrong people. I know this one thing to be true. Love, real love, is only found in Christ. No matter what flower you pick out of the garden, or how many petals that you must weed out, the end result will always be the same, God loves you! He loved me through hard times. He loves you the same. He loved me through my disobedience. He loves you the same. He loved me through my pride. He loves you the same. I'm not thirsting for love, because God loves me enough. He loves you the same. He loves us always and forever and commands us to DO the same. You can be a great person, deliver a great speech, and donate a lot of money but if you really want to leave a lasting impact on someone, love them.   People will know that you are a child of God just by your love!

Study Your Scripture:

John 15:9-17, NIV

"As the Father has loved me, so have I loved you. Now remain in my love. If you keep my commands, you will remain in my love, just as I have kept my Father's commands and remain in his love. I have told you this so that my joy may be in you and that your joy may be complete. My command is this: Love each other as I have loved you. Greater love has no one than this: to lay down one's life for one's friends. You are my friends if you do what I command. I no longer call you servant because a servant does not know his master's business. Instead, I have called you friends, for everything that I learned from my Father I have made known to you. You did not choose me, but I chose you and appointed you so that you might go and bear fruit—fruit that will last—and so that whatever you ask in my name the Father will give you. This is my command: Love each other."

Sing Your Song:

"You" by Jermaine Dolly

Tell Your Tale:

What was your favorite childhood game? Share the details of the first day that you fell in love with Jesus.

_____

_____

_____

_____

_____

_____

_____

_____

_____

_____

_____

_____

_____

_____

_____

_____

_____

Love Without Judgment

Maybe it's just me, but sometimes people really irk me. You know who I'm referring to, people, God's children. I understand that we were all created in His image, and everything He made was good. I try not to judge, become easily frustrated, or respond to those people who just have a problem with life. But in all honesty, I fail a lot. My patience is thumbtack sharp and short for those who are selfish, negative, and disturbers of the peace. Some people have learned to cast their load on God, while others are still trying to work it out alone, that's such a big mistake. When people choose to live without God's directions, those negative characteristics easily slip out.

What can we do to make life better when dealing with "those folks?"

First things first. Remember, that at some point, you were "those folks." Truth be told, you may still be one of "those folks." Some days, I am still "those folks." In the book of Romans, Paul reminds the Romans that no one is righteous, and all have sinned and fallen short. It is only by God's grace and our faith in Him that we are made whole and justified. As a people, we are not to judge another but to encourage, teach, and help them along the way. Paul addresses the Romans as the beloved of God, called to be saints (Romans 1:7). Informally, the word saint means to be a loving, kind, and patient person trying to live holy. Here's the spoiler alert: we have that same calling on us, so we must "Therefore receive one another

just as Christ has received us, to the glory of God."
(Romans 15:7) It is incumbent upon us that we
receive others with the love of God. We are to lead
them to our Heavenly Father who has saved us
from all sin. Remember, the best leaders lead by
example.

Here's my truth: I'm still growing. Some of
my fruits are in full bloom, while others are just
budding. But I'm growing. I often remind myself
that when I'm judgmental, selfish, negative, and
just plain worrisome, God loves me anyway. I was
doing the best that I could, at that moment.
People are often doing the best that they can. Love
them through all their stuff and watch God make
a change in them. There will also be a change in
you for the better. After all, you are called to be a
saint.

Study Your Scripture:

Romans 15:1-6, NIV

"We who are strong ought to bear with the failings of the weak and not to please ourselves. Each of us should please our neighbors for their good, to build them up. For even Christ did not please himself but, as it is written: "The insults of those who insult you have fallen on me." For everything that was written in the past was written to teach us, so that through the endurance taught in the Scriptures and the encouragement they provide we might have hope. May the God who gives endurance and encouragement give you the same attitude of mind toward each other that Christ Jesus had, so that with one mind and one voice you may glorify the God and Father of our Lord

Jesus Christ. Accept one another, then, just as Christ accepted you, in order to bring praise to God. "

Sing Your Song:

"I Need You to Survive" by Hezekiah Walker

Tell Your Tale:

Name a personality trait of a friend or family member that bothers you at times. What steps do you take to look past that bothersome trait and love your Christian brother or sister anyhow?

_____

_____

_____

_____

_____

_____

_____

_____

_____

_____

_____

_____

_____

_____

I Love God

In the year 2015, a popular female gospel artist pinned a song entitled, "I Love God." In the song, the singer questions her audience. She speaks of all the many reasons that she loves God, and then she ponders aloud if we love God too. Those two questions and a statement should help you get yourself together with God immediately. I love God because He first loved me. I love God because He has kept me. I love God because He protects me. I love God because He knows me. I love God because He directs me. Before I was even thought about, He died to save me. I love God. Do you love God?

Everything that He did for me was done for you as well. If you are not able to see the reason to love and serve God, the next question is most important for your salvation. What's wrong with you? Take a moment and think about what your life would look like had it not been for Christ's ultimate sacrifice. Would you still be wandering in Egypt? Would you still be sinning in Sodom? Would you still be depending upon the priests to sacrifice and plead for forgiveness on your behalf? Christ changed the trajectory of your life so that you could have a chance at living life abundantly. He has put the laws in our hearts and wrote them in our minds because He desires for us to spend life eternally with Him. His death was part of the plan for our salvation. When we submit to His will, His love will flow freely. If you choose to reject the knowledge of God's word, there is no other sacrifice that can be found. Do not make the mistake of giving in to your own sinful desires and having to wait in fear and expectation of the wrath of God. In God, there is no gray area. There are no bounds to His love. You are His child, an heir of the Kingdom. You were bought with a hefty price, the Perfect Lamb of God. My grandma used to say, "When you know better, you should do better." Remember, God loved us first.

Study Your Scripture:

John 3:16-21, NIV

"For God so loved the world that he gave his one and only Son, that whoever believes in him shall not perish but have eternal life. For God did not send his Son into the world to condemn the world, but to save the world through him. Whoever believes in him is not condemned, but whoever does not believe stands condemned already because they have not believed in the name of God's one and only Son. This is the verdict: Light has come into the world, but people loved darkness instead of light because their deeds were evil. Everyone who does evil hates the light and will not come into the light for fear that their deeds will be exposed. But whoever lives by the truth comes into the light, so that it may be seen plainly that what they have done has been done in the sight of God."

Sing Your Song:

"I Love God" by Erica Campbell

Tell Your Tale:

Describe your love for God. When did you first experience the depth of God's love?

_____

_____

_____

_____

_____

_____

_____

_____

_____

_____

_____

_____

_____

_____

_____

_____

_____

_____

_____

Love Paid In Full

Jesus paid it all. Why are we running on "E"? There is nothing in Christ that we should want and not be able to receive. The price was paid for all our troubles, transgressions, tribulations, trials, and trespasses with Jesus' death on the cross. His life was the ransom which would allow us to live life and live it more abundantly. His bruises and scars paid for it all. The chastisements of our sins were upon Him. He took our issues as His own. The beatings that we deserved; Jesus took instead. The lies that should have been placed on us were placed with the crown of thorns on His head. The shame of what felt and even looked like defeat, He endured. The rejection from friends was disappointing, yet, he stayed the course. The backstabbing, He saw it. With this realization, our love tank should never be empty. With His life, Jesus paid for **EVERYTHING** in full. Jesus paid it all for us; so our problems, our mistakes, our sins, our issues, our disappointments, our decisions, and our attitude would not cost us our lives. He handled the requirements for eternity so that we could live life with the promise of a new earth with Him and His father, for always.

As an heir of the Kingdom and a child of God, yours is the kingdom of heaven. Life is meant to be lived, so why are you trudging along without energy, purpose, or passion? Why is your tank on "E" when everything that you need to survive and thrive is available to you? If you do not know how to access what's yours, turn to Matthew 7:8 and find these words,

"Everyone who asks receives what he asks for. Everyone who looks finds what he is looking for. Everyone who knocks has the door opened to him." God's love is everlasting. We used to sing a song when I was little that spoke of God's riches. The song declared that God would do it all if we only followed one direction. We must trust in Him. God can raise the dead, heal the sick, provide houses, and land. All that is required of us is to trust and believe. Each day, check-in with God to keep your tank full. His ultimate gift of Love on the cross has paid your way from here unto eternity. Keep going, don't push the brake or accelerate the gas. You won't run out of God's love. He will carry you all the way.

Study Your Scripture:

1 John 4:7-21, NIV

"Dear friends, let us love one another, for love comes from God. Everyone who loves has been born of God and knows God. Whoever does not love does not know God, because God is love. This is how God showed his love among us: He sent his one and only Son into the world that we might live through him. This is love: not that we loved God, but that he loved us and sent his Son as an atoning sacrifice for our sins. Dear friends, since God so loved us, we also ought to love one another. No one has ever seen God; but if we love one another, God lives in us and his love is made complete in us.

This is how we know that we live in him and he in us: He has given us of his Spirit. And we have seen and testify that the Father has sent his Son to be the Savior of the world. If anyone acknowledges that Jesus is the Son of God, God lives in them and they in God. And so we know and rely on the love God has for us. God is love. Whoever lives in love lives in God, and God in them. This is how love is made complete among us so that we will have confidence on the day of judgment: In this world we are like Jesus. There is no fear in love. But perfect love drives out fear because fear has to do with punishment. The one who fears is not made perfect in love. We love because he first loved us. Whoever claims to love God yet hates a brother or sister is a liar. For whoever does not love their brother and sister, whom they have seen, cannot love God, whom they have not seen. And he has

given us this command: Anyone who loves God

must also love their brother and sister."

Sing Your Song:

"No Greater Love" by GMWA Mass Choir

Tell Your Tale:

Do you feel worthy of God's love? How can you explain God's love to nonbelievers?

_____
_____
_____
_____
_____
_____
_____
_____
_____
_____
_____
_____
_____
_____
_____
_____
_____
_____
_____

Run Straight Into His Loving Arms

We've all gotten off track at least one time. We've said a few choice words and may have done some ungodly things. We danced at the club late on a Saturday night and praised God early on a Sunday morning. We've straddled the fence, Jesus on one side, the world on the other. We know that God's way is the best way but some of our behaviors, we feel, just cannot be forgiven. Our life may be filled with stuff, but we are still empty and yearning to be fulfilled with the love that only God can provide. We know our lives can be better if we only go back to our start, to our Maker, to our Creator. Have you made your way back? If not, what's stopping you? Have you made too many mistakes? Have you told too many lies and hurt too many people? Have you been "in the world" for too long? If that's your case, find comfort in these words. Do not allow yourself to be so ashamed that you feel your sinful behaviors are unforgivable. Turn to God! He is always ready to welcome you back home in the beat of His heart and the bosom of His arms. The truth is you are never too far gone.

In the book of Luke 15, there is a popular parable of the lost son. His father gave him his lot in life. He decided to move from under his father's rules and travel through life alone. In the beginning, he had a great time. He partied and spent all his inheritance on loose living. He had plenty of joys, but pain was not far ahead. A famine came across the land and he was in need.

Although he should've been prepared, he had nothing. No one helped him. He had no covering from his father. Eventually, he returned home. The poor prodigal son did not know what to expect back home but he came with a repentant heart and an open mind. He knew that life with his father was better than life on his own. When he was a way off from his home, his father saw him and began to run towards him. He wanted to welcome his son home in a grand fashion. He asked his servants to get him the best robe and to prepare the greatest feast, for this was a celebration. His son had finally returned home.

Do you believe that God loves you the same way? Even when He sees you in pain and in bad situations, it hurts Him, yet He waits on you. He waits on your call and then He comes running.

He is eager, willing, and ready to hold you in His arms. His love will melt all the pain away. If you have called on God, meet Him in the gap. You know He's coming; run towards Him.

Study Your Scripture:

Luke 15:11-20, NIV

"Jesus continued: "There was a man who had two sons. The younger one said to his father, 'Father, give me my share of the estate.' So he divided his property between them. "Not long after that, the younger son got together all he had, set off for a distant country and there squandered his wealth in wild living. After he had spent everything, there was a severe famine in that whole country, and he began to be in need. So he went and hired himself out to a citizen of that country, who sent him to his fields to feed pigs. He longed to fill his stomach with the pods that the pigs were eating, but no one gave him anything. "When he came to his senses, he said, 'How many of my father's hired servants have food to spare, and here I am starving to death! I will set out and go back to my father and say to him: Father, I have sinned against heaven and against you. I am no longer worthy to be called your son; make me like one of your hired servants.' So he got up and went to his father. But while he was still a long way off, his father saw him and was filled with compassion for him; he ran to his son, threw his arms around him, and kissed him."

Sing Your Song:

"Respond" by Travis Greene

Tell Your Tale:

Why do you think it is so difficult for the current church to maintain the membership of the younger generation? If you have turned away from God, what is hindering you from seeking Him again?

_____
_____
_____
_____
_____
_____
_____
_____
_____
_____
_____
_____
_____
_____
_____

Dear God, the Lover of my Soul,

God, you are awesome and mighty in Your ways. Yet, I often struggle to conceptualize how great Your love is for me. You loved me before I was born. You loved me in my brokenness. You loved me through my troubles. When I needed a reminder of Your love, You sent me a beautiful sunrise, Your most perfect artwork for the day. Thank You, God. Yet, my Father, You knew I needed more. You then sent me the most beautiful ballad sung by two little bluebirds nesting on my front porch. Although I smiled, God, by Your infinite wisdom and understanding of me, You knew I still needed more. I thank You, God. Then, You sent a long-lost friend my way to tell me that, although we are far away, she still thinks of me, loves me, and cherishes our fun times together. You wanted me to know that You love me like that but even a little bit more. Thank You, Father God, I now understand. You love me too much to focus on my past mistakes. You desire to love me now, into the future, and forevermore. I'm back at home in Your arms. I'd hoped that I would be welcome, and You welcomed me. Lord, therefore, I am comfortable and at peace. I've overcome many problems; I know that more may arise. But today, I'm freed from past hurt and pain. Lord, I am safe with You. But above all, God, I am loved by You and I love You too. With endless love and a thankful heart always.

In Jesus' name, I pray, Amen.

Made in the USA
Columbia, SC
02 August 2020

14259434R00104